Short Skirts and Whiskey Shots
Tales of nights I shouldn't have made it home alive

Published by Earth Island Books
Pickforde Lodge
Pickforde Lane
Ticehurst
East Sussex
TN5 7BN

www.earthislandbooks.com

First published by Earth Island Books 2023

ISBN 9781739443801

Printed and bound by Solopress

Short Skirts and Whiskey Shots

Tales of nights I shouldn't have made it home alive

A Fifth Floor Walk-Up

Westchester to the Lower East Side

This is what adults call a transition period.

My last semester at SUNY Purchase
        with an apartment in Alphabet City
                and a reverse commute to Westchester.

Twenty years old
        with no marketable skills
                nor the luxury of accepting a day job.

Armed with one summer at a small town pizza shop,
        a skirt just short enough,
         and as much charm and confidence as I can rally,

I take my resume
        to every bar, diner, café, and fast food joint
                in the Lower East Side, the East Village, and Greenwich Village.

Managers graciously accept copies
    which I assume are promptly pitched in the nearest trash can
        because I only ever get one call back.

I somehow managed to fake my way
        into a shift at Around the Clock
                and my new life, in New York City.

10th Street and Avenue B

This apartment is the type of place
    you can only live in your 20s
        when you are young, broke, and stupid.

Alphabet City
    with no grocery store
        or subway nearby.

Avenue B
    near Tompkins Square Park
        two doors down from the Life Café.

A fifth-floor walk-up
    without an air conditioner or a cross breeze
        and baseboard heat that doesn't work.

A glorified studio
    billed as a one bedroom
        with a kitchen too small to cook in.

300 square feet
    with a television on the floor
        and fabric masquerading as curtains masquerading as doors.

A pre-law tenement
    with a toilet room, a tuberculous window,
        and a fire escape with roof access.

It is tiny.
    It is run-down.
        It is mine.

Avenue B, 2004

These first nights are hard —
                no family or friends,
                no familiar faces,
                no cable or internet,
                    alone in a new city
                        of strangers.

Watching Empire Records on repeat
      on a TV that sits on the floor.
Listening to scratched records
    I found in front of St. Mark's Church.

Late at night, I go to the roof —
stare at the city
                building lights,
                silhouettes in windows,
                cars on the streets
watch the stoplight
                in front of the bodega on 10th and B
                change for hours
listen as laughter rises
                from Life Café's garden—
knowing I don't belong to any of it.

And once a week, on Tuesdays,
      I call my boyfriend,
      a million miles and light years away, in Philly,
                              let the loneliness spill out.

Around the Clock

My first day at Around the Clock
I meet a vegan punk rock kid
     wearing too-tight jeans, worn-out Converse,
        and a Ramones button on his apron next to the
           crusty carrot ginger dressing stain.

I trail Tight Pants,
     memorizing the menu and
        the arbitrary table number system.

He introduces me to the regulars
     as if we have been friends for years.
I even get a few phone numbers,
        offers to show me around.

That night, we walk around the city –
     Tight Pants trying his best to impress.
       We walk from the East Village
                       to Battery Park
               to the Meatpacking District
            to Times Square
        to the Upper East Side
     and back to my Alphabet City apartment
to watch the sunrise on my roof.

As the sky slowly turns pink,
     for the first time
       I feel like this is real
         like I really did it
           Like I am really
                 here.

From Battery Park to the Upper East Side

Staying up all night
    always creates
        a sort of —
            enchantment.
The air changes
    as the sky begins to lighten.
        The inside knowledge
            of a quiet world
                just waking up,
                    becoming conscious of itself again.

Those liminal minutes -
    before the sounds of the day,
        before the rush hour horns,
            before the shouting voices
                heighten every nerve.

This is the time -
        when we swear we can fly -
            when poems are born -
                when paintings are sketched -
                    when symphonies are composed -
                        when we are captivated.

Tompkins Square Park

I swear it has been summer
        for twelve months now.
90 degrees in the shade and
        through the night.

The fifth floor is a furnace.
The window is open
        but there is no opportunity
            for a cross-breeze.

Sans air conditioning
sans cable, sans curtains
I find solace in the East Village.

Still not 21, I spend my Friday nights
wandering through the streets
        from Avenue B to Astor Place
            from Union Square and Houston.

I walk past Tompkins Square Park to Key Foods
barely making it back up the five flights
        plastic grocery bags digging into my arms
            packed with generic bread, cereal, peanut butter.

I can connect to the public Wi-Fi,
        if I sit on my fire escape.
Log in to LiveJournal and AIM,
        talk with friends from back home
            who are now scattered all over the world.

Everything is changing
        right at the moment
            my life is beginning.

I am not ready for any of it
        yet burning to start,
            tired of stalling.

These hot summer nights on Avenue B
        are perfectly humid
            perfectly still
                perfectly alive.

162 Avenue B

Ever since I was a kid, I wanted a balcony.
                                I spend hours suspended above the city,
                    on my fire escape on Avenue B.
A cardboard box lines the wrought iron floor,
            my back against the brick wall,
                        Converse pushed against the railing,
                            a notebook propped against knees.
                                I soak in the neighborhood,
                                    listen to voices float up,
                                        becoming only murmurs after
                                                    five stories.
I watch waitresses and bartenders
        walk to their shifts,
businessmen
        drop off laundry in the morning
                pick up perfectly folded cubes on their way home,
firemen come and go,
        yet I never see the same one start then finish a shift,
tourists search for street signs, and
        drunks laugh a bit too loud.

My favorite though,
        is the clanking of silverware and glasses,
                voices and laughter merge
                    and rise like a ball
                        of energy from the Life Café's garden.

7B

The table is cluttered is with empty beer pints
          and towers of rocks glasses –
              sticky, dripping with Jameson.
An old friend is in town,
          one I've missed for years.

We are at one of my usual dives,
          the one with the photo booth and
              best jukebox in New York City.

We sing along to the songs
          we screamed along to in high school.
The songs that still mean so much,
        yet mean something different now.

Our sweaters and hoodies are draped over
          the backs of chairs;
the air inside the bar is so thick
        the windows fog over
          so densely we can't see
        that it has stopped snowing outside.

The sheet of photo booth pictures –
          our arms around each other laughing,
              sticking out our tongues,
                  flashing the horns.
Forgetting the time and the distance that separate
        who we are
              from who we used to be.

North of 29th Street at 2 am

It isn't raining anymore.
    It is more of a mist –
        like the sky is spitting at
            New York City.

Forty-seven degrees feels like spring
    compared to the freezing temperatures
        we've been trapped by for months.

It is only 2 am –
    we don't want to stay at the bar
        and we don't want to go home.

The city is alive,
    and we sleep through it too often.

We start walking north,
    not knowing where we will arrive.

42nd Street at 3 am

I only love Times Square at 3 am –
    when the theaters on Broadway are dark,
        the tourists are tucked back in their hotel rooms and
            the drunks are still at the bars –
                when the nut and pretzel vendors linger
                   and the pigeons and rats mark their territory.

I love the lights that never dim.
    Three in the morning is just as bright as noon.
        The blues and reds and purples
            reflect off the empty sidewalks,
                bounce from the glass and chrome buildings,
                   flicker on our faces.

Stuyvesant Street

Everyone huddles inside Around the Clock
      nursing cups of coffee, reading,
      staring at the rain outside.
Hidden behind a computer screen,
      writing, I listen to the murmur of low music
      and quiet voices.
The dampness seeps up the leg of my jeans.

People rush in
      hunched over,
            with rain-speckled shoulders.

A man in sweatpants
      paces under the awning
       chain smoking
           as the rain ricochets off
            garbage bags.

A cab splashes
      a woman in a suit walking
           a dog in a raincoat.

Umbrellas gush inside out.

No one sits
      on the benches of St. Mark's Church.

The streetlights reflect
      off the soaked roads.

Buses, cabs, and cars
      headlights, taillights, stoplights,
       strobe against the slick macadam.

WALK/DONT WALK
      flashes on the corner.

Outside the rain stops,
     but the wind still gusts
       the bottom of my jeans are still wet,

                        Manhattan is saturated.

Opaline

New York City, you are the most enthralling
        at your rawest moments.
            In your underground bars,
                with your beautiful freaks,
                    with your endearing misfits,
                        with your experimental artists.
                            and unrestrained spectators.

Your East Village held onto the 90s –
    it remains the dirty, artistic, rebellious,
                community-driven, demanding creative freedom,
                    and acceptance while pushing boundaries,
                        because the world can fucking explode tonight –
                                    even after the millennium broke.

That basement on Avenue A
        where murals painted in DayGlo paint
                explode under the black lights.
                    A Clockwork Orange or vintage porn
                                plays on a loop
                            on the screens behind the bar
                      and surrounding the dance floor.
                Go-go dancers and drag queens
            always reign supreme.
        Stunning men and women dance
    in cages on the bar
with all their androgynous magnetism.

The weekly panties party
    always draws a crowd—
        cheap drinks
            boys and girls and non-binary beauties
                in tighty-whities and tube socks
                jockstraps and pasties.

Sweat and glitter stick to every surface.
    It is an American Apparel ad waiting to happen.
        It is innocent.
            It is freedom.
                It is ours.

                Until the hipsters bring it all to Brooklyn
                      and sell it to the highest bidder.

Niagara

I am not your prey
        nor your conquest.

Just because my skirt is short
        doesn't mean that I am looking
                for someone to take me home.

I am here to drink and laugh
        and catch up with old friends.

Generally, all things that don't involve you
        stepping in the middle of our conversation.

I am not impressed by how much you make,
        or your clothes, or your job, or your car.

I'll judge you by your drink
        and what song you put on the jukebox.

I will go shot for shot,
        and no, I don't want you to buy me one.

I am not leaving with you.
        I am going home with my friends tonight.

We are going to blast some Against Me!
        and lay on the roof looking over Avenue B.

NY, NY

We each live
      in a secluded world
           alongside   so many people.

No contact, words, or smiles.
    Stare straight ahead —
      look like you have somewhere you
         should have been ten minutes ago.

Sunglasses obscure
      your eyes,
headphones block
      out
        voices, horns,
           birds, construction -
every sound the city throws at you
         to assert her voice.

Strive for your own space.
    Savor the six inches around your path.

The constant threat of interaction
      forces you to develop your own unique
        defense mechanisms.
Fighting,
    for that single moment
        that is yours
          alone.

The 6 Local

You are not a real New Yorker
    until you become one with the subway.

Swipe your MetroCard,
    run down the stairs,
        Snake around the slow movers
            just in case you have to jump in through the already-closing doors.

Try to gauge when the last train was here
        by how many people are on the platform.
            Listen in the distance for the hum.
                Squint to see the headlights.

Learn the maps,
    the routes,
     the stops.

Know the hubs.
    Know where you can transfer
        to a crosstown train.
    Know the transfers that take you blocks
        before you realize that it would have been faster
                or at least less murder-y above ground.

Careen with the train.
    Hold onto the bar
        lock your knees
            let your hips sway
                so you won't stumble
                    (it is all core work).

Learn to speak conductor.
    It requires a good ear and
        the ability to pattern match.

Know if your train is an express or local.
   Listen for route changes –
        for locals instantly becoming expresses.

Don't get trapped on the wrong side of the train.
    Stand in the doorway.
        Get off and on if you have to.
           Don't get pushed into the middle.
             Make your way to the door
                at least one stop before you have to get off.

Ignore the performers
    but always think to yourself,
        you admire them,
            just a bit.

Except for the mariachi bands,
a subway car is way too confined
for that level of sound.

And never.
I mean never.
Under any circumstance.
Never.
Get into an empty subway car.

Cherry Tavern

In a post-break-up-reckless-self-destructive period,
        I meet him.
He is in a band that used to play in my hometown
        when I was in high school.

He has always looked too clean-cut to be in a punk band.
        His older brother was the punk rock heartthrob,
                every girl in the scene crushed on when we were sixteen.

Crutches or escapes,
        or a bit of both
                is what we really are for one another.
Never serious,
        our whole relationship
                (I suppose you can call it a relationship, of sorts)
                        is drinking and sex.
                                Mostly messy-not-good-half-remembered-drunk sex.

There is one night,
        some time that first winter,
                after we started dating
                        (I suppose you could call it dating)
in Cherry Tavern
        when he puts *Into the Great Wide Open*
                on the jukebox.

And I think,
        even just for these three minutes
                and forty-five seconds.
                That maybe,
                        maybe this can become something more.

Boy's Room

We are at a Burning Angel party
    at Boy's Room.
The bar already has a stripper pole
    and is packed with tattooed, pierced, Manic Panic
    Rainbow-colored art students, freaks, and artists.
        I have never felt so plain,
            so bland, so invisible in my whole life.

Joanna Angel is performing,
    her tiny tattooed frame
        athletically spinning around the pole,
            commanding the room as she dances.
        Entrepreneur porn star,
    she found a missing market segment
        and filled it,
        building an alternative empire.

The bartender serves drinks wearing gold short shorts
    à la Rocky in Rocky Horror Picture Show
        complete with blond hair and greased abs.

A drag queen, Peppermint
        takes the stage,
            performs her ass off
                shows up everyone –
                        the porn star, the buff bartender, the gogo dancers
                        but in all fairness, Boy's Room is her turf.

As she exits
    she grabs my face
        calls me gorgeous
            and walks away.

West 4 St – Washington Sq Station

The rush hour train
      packed with commuters
           all in a hurry
                to get somewhere they don't want to be,
        becomes a mosh pit
      of bodies compressed
jockeying for their places,
      moving as one mass
         as they lurch
                    between stops.
Aggressive energy defends each spot.
      Feet planted firmly,
             prepared to throw a jab if needed
You may think you are safe
         on the outskirts,
                but you may catch a stray elbow.

The night train
      seems melancholy without its commuters.
        It is now a shoegaze show
           with voids of space on the floor in between swaying bodies
              that barely notice as the train slides into the stations.
        Its steady rhythm soothes,
       the rocking motion that makes you forget
      the chaos right above your head.

Center of the Universe

Surge with the city.
        Feel the pulse.
                Live in moments.

Work premiere parties.
      Go to shows.
            Crash events.
                Brunch on Sundays afternoons
                        through dark sunglasses.

Sleep is for the weak.
      Apartments are claustrophobic anyway.
            Roam the streets until dawn.
                Come home with the sunrise.

Write in cafés.
      Meet friends for dinner in trendy restaurants.
            Waste the night in a dive bar.
            Move forward.

TV is background noise as you crash.
      The subway can take you anywhere.
            You never need to leave Manhattan.

Indulge – cook dinner and spend a night in.
      Never go to the grocery store.
            Shop at the bodega across the street.

Watch tourists pose for photos,
      translate maps,
            and try to decipher the poet
                from the drug addict at St. Mark's Church.

Sit on a fire escape.
      Sit in a coffee shop.
            Sit in a bar.

Watch all the people rush,
      residents mix with tourists,
            the city is always moving.

Realize this is your life.
      You live here.

Times Square

It is our tradition –

Wake up way too early
    when the bums are still passed out
        in Tompkins Square Park,
            the line at Amor Bakery
                hasn't even started to form,
                  Union Square is quiet,
                      skaters and college students still
                        sleeping off their weeks,
                just a few old men and women feed
                  stale bread to the pigeons.
                  It is the only time you can hear
                    the subway roll into the stop
                        from the sidewalk. The methodical
                          metal pattern dissipates into the air
                            with no voices to override the sound.
                            Catch the N/R/W to Times Square
                            and get off at the 42nd street stop.
Plow through the masses of people.   Sweaty, fighting against the crowd
Approaching the 4th circle of hell   or Times Square as it is better known.
        Vendors are setting   up, throngs of people exit their hotel rooms
                stare up at buildings   not knowing what direction they need to go.
The noise of conversations   and sales barkers are already at a deafening decibel.
Virgin, Billabong,   Planet Hollywood, the Hard Rock Café
have already opened.   Their doors wide and beckoning.
Shoulder check,   bob and weave through the crowd.
The constant   surge of people going in opposite directions.
Push forward   and back.
        Pass the   knock-off   purses, sunglasses, and watches,
          merchandise   on a tarp   that can easily be torn down and packed up
            in an instant   Pass the legit pashmina vendors and souvenir stores,
               Sponge   Bobs, Elmos, and girls in pasties.
              Pass the nut   and pretzel vendors with their wafting sugar,
                    for the chance to score
                      student rush lottery tickets
                        to a Broadway play.

Finally, reach the theater.
        Mom is already in line
            with a cup of coffee.

Colony Records

The neon sign beckons from blocks away.
Walking into Colony Records
is like going to a museum,
but entry is free and you can buy the exhibits.

When you walk through the doors
adorned with gilded treble clefs,
you step into the past—
a bygone era that you never lived.

The Brill building made it through
the seedy days of Times Square.
Musicians, singers, and performers—
    Carol King, Bobby Darin, The Shirelles, The Shangri-Las,
    the Ronettes, Frankie Valli and the 4 Seasons, Liza Minelli, The Drifters
each offered a note, a line, a melody, a single to its story.

Look up-down-left-and-right to take it all in.
Albums cover every square inch of the walls,
racks of posters, shelves of sheet music, bins of CDs
all expertly squeezed into this footprint while
avoiding the water damage on the back wall.

Tourists mix with regulars, the frazzled musician searches
for a tune he only half remembers; a collector looking to uncover
something she doesn't know is missing from her collection.

It doesn't matter how many times I go,
I still ogle everything like I am seeing it for the first time.
The cases of music memorabilia that I can't afford –
Beatles pins, flags, combs, magazines. Elvis, the Who, the Monkees,
back before merchandise was officially licensed. Imagining
what it will be like to be able to own, just one piece of this place one day.

I thread up and down each aisle,
tripping and banging my knees
when I take a turn too tight.

I never tire of running my hands
over all the history contained within these walls.

Alphabet City

We walk these streets every day, every night, every morning.
Hell, we own these streets.

We know the location of every photo booth
    from Houston to 21st street
       from B to Broadway.
          (And which are digital
                    and which are old school film,
                       bonus points for Lakeside who still uses tokens.)

We know the bars that aren't crowded on a Saturday night,
    the ones with the heavy pours,
       the ones where you can get a drink after 4 am.

There are nights of board games at HiFi,
    $5 shots of tequila with a Tecate backer at Cherry Tavern,
       pool at Ace,
          darts at Blue and Gold,
             punk rock at 7B,
                hipsters at Manitoba's.

We know when you go to dinner at 3 am, 7A's nachos are unrivaled.
    We know when you go to Ray's on A for the milkshakes
       you also get a sidewalk full of drunks telling slurred stories
          trying to sober up on greasy Belgian fries.

You go to Sidewalk and Life for a cheap bunch,
    shows at the Knitting Factory and Arlene's Grocery,
       and Red Bamboo for the best vegan wings and fish sticks.

We always walk home from work, taking the long way –
    Chelsea through Union Square to the East Village,
       give all the kitchen leftovers to the homeless we pass,
          wander in and out of community gardens,
             run through sprinklers in Stuyvesant Town.
               Our voices carry through the 5 am streets.

These streets host
    2 am visits for coffee at Yaffa,
       3 am writing sessions paired with pierogi at Veselka,
          4 am calls when the bars are closing
             and the PATH stops running, or the trek to Brooklyn is just too much.
               It doesn't matter, we always have floor space.

No matter what time of day
    or night
       or early morning
          the streets are busy
            the streets are alive
             the streets are ours.

A Love Letter to the 2 Avenue Station F/V

I've been in quite a few subway stations,
        but you,
                Second Avenue, are...

                                    ...unique.
                                ...one of a kind.
                    ...like nothing I've ever experienced.
                ...a portal to hell?

Really, it's almost as if your air
        has been replaced
                by already inhaled bad breath
                        that our lungs are incapable of re-breathing in.

You are somehow
        electrified by the third rail
                until the atmosphere is boiled in the urine
                        emanating from the walls and the floor and the ceiling.

You are defiant.
        Protesting the closing of the city's grimy dives,
                its ethnic groceries,
                        its all -night bodegas.

You are fighting.
      Resisting the luxury hotels,
         the high-rise apartments,
            the high-end boutiques.

You are proud of your dirty
        clandestine past.

You don't feel the need to be scrubbed
        or whitewashed.

You, Second Avenue F/V stop,
                are the last to say,
                    "Give me your tired,

                              your poor,
                                        your huddled masses yearning..."

14th Street – Union Square Station

Station after station
    of unmanned ticket booths
        MetroCard swipes unlock another world.

The performers, dancers, musicians,
      the bootleg DVD peddlers,
           the evangelical pamphleteers who are dedicated
                to convert all the New York heathens as they rush
      home from their soul-suffocating jobs.

Lean against the door
      balance
read *Howl* for the third time this week.

A Forfeited Security Deposit

Chelsea Billiards

As I walk through that heavy glass door
      I know I am entering a different stratum of NYC.
                                   Of my life.

It is cold.
    Metallic.
        Grey.
            Modern.

The DJ booth looms over an empty dance floor.
      French fries are served in sculptures of modern art.
           LEDs light up the vacant glass-topped bar.
                Chrome tables sit empty.

Sleek and impersonal,
      but in a way that is incredibly on-trend.

Waiters and waitresses all in black.
      All young.
           All beautiful.
                All too manicured for 10 am
                        on a Sunday morning brunch.

I shift.
           Rock on the outside soles of my Chucks.
           Wonder how I can ever pass.

12 Blocks North, 6 Blocks West

Snatched from working an overnight shift at Around the Clock,
    an all-night diner on Stuyvesant and Broadway.

I travel uptown and west, to Slate,
    a Chelsea pool hall that desperately wants to be a club.

Baptized by fire, my first table is Mila Kunis, Seth Green, and Colin Hanks –
    You got here ten minutes ago, don't fuck up.

I master the menu, the bar list, and the POS software,
    all I need to do is prove I can hang.

My first shift drink order, a Jameson, neat.
        It was a test.
                I pass.

We become a crew.
        Work shifts together. Party together.
                Only separating as we stumble home at six in the morning.

The ones who come in,
        work their shift,
                then go home,
                        never seem to last.

Movie premieres, fashion shows, wrap parties—
    serve, drink, dates with celebrities,
        phone numbers written on checks
            with big tips attached.

Our corporate parties invite us to drink with them.
    let them into our world,
        even if only for the night.
    Everyone accepting our challenge—
        keep up if you want to hang with us.

There are nights we can't see straight enough to do our closeouts.
        Nights we stumble into the Christmas tree.
            Nights we dance on stage.
                Nights we never stop.

Slate, 5 pm

The summer day cut
        off
as the doors close
        behind me.

Humidity, air, sunlight,
        swallowed
                into the artificially
                        cool interior
                                of dim light and stone floors.
The cold draft
        of the air conditioning carries
                the smell of stale vodka and beer
                        through the empty club.

The radio's echo
        falls hollow,
                the empty voices
                        seem to know they have
                                no audience.

The building is
        a skeleton of what
                it will become
                        in a few hours.

Girls in black
        skirts, heels, and tank tops
                prep for tonight –
        roll sliver, cut fruit, wipe down tables,
                as a few happy hour businessmen,
                        loosen their ties and tip badly.

It won't be until after midnight
        the alcohol gives life to
                sweaty bodies and sloppy performances.

Brunch at the Life Café

Twenty-two years old.
  So certain of the world
    and my place in it.

Young, pretty, and on the inside,
  and so are my friends.

We own New York City,
  or at least think we do.

We are an exclusive club
  and we aren't looking for new members.

We sit in dark dives during the day,
  work in trendy clubs at night,
    drink in after-hours bars,
      and meet for brunch at noon.

Through dark sunglasses,
  over bloody marys,
    and a pitcher of water
      at a Life Café brunch
        we recount and fill in
          missing moments of the night before.

We laugh as we
  hydrate our hangovers,
    never looking one another in the eye.

Lakeside Lounge

Sit in a bar
        dark at noon.

Read page after page
        of classic literature
                supplemented by the Beats
                        and punk rock historians.

Search for inspiration.
        Search for my authentic voice.

The City that Never Sleeps

Manhattan is a nocturnal animal
    full of day sleepers and night shift workers.

In the daylight,
    the garbage permeates
        and the buildings throw
            menacing shadows.

The neon behind tinted glass fights the morning sun,
    the air conditioning lingers in the doorways,
        the stale smell of beer and liquor hover.

The city hums
    waiting for the sun to go down,
        waiting to beckon,
            waiting to saturate.

54 West 21st Street

Waiter, waitress, cocktail waitress, server
    call me whatever you want,
        I don't mind, it treats me well.

It's a job that doesn't require a college degree
    (as most jobs that end at 4 am don't)
        but I need proficiency in psychology,
            street smarts, acting, ballet, and charisma.
    I have mastered them all.

Flirt.
    Keep them interested.
        Keep them here.
            Keep them ordering top shelf.

Maneuver trays full of martinis
    across a dance floor
        to
        packed pool tables.
Arch your back
    raise your arm to avoid
        a careless pool cue
            or a hand trying to grab your attention
                only to order another Stella.

Smile.
    Flirt more.
        Give him a fake phone number.
            Or better yet, a fictitious jealous boyfriend.
                Toss out the phone number, keep the cash.
            Always get 20%
        or more.

By close
    they will all become blurry faces
        wild hands
            failing livers
                and rent checks.

Just another Wednesday Night on 21st Street

It happens more often than you imagine.
>Usually, on a slow night with a bar full of tourists
>>looking to escape their comfort zone
>>>in front of an audience they will never see again.

Samba, always the instigator
>wipes down the bar,
>>with a mischievous smile.

It only takes a few drinks and just enough protest
>for her to take on the role,
>>using peer pressure as an excuse
>>>to climb on the bar.

It is always a girl,
>slightly self-conscious,
>>secretly wanting to let go,
>>>to become the object of desire,
>>>>surrounded by friends.
>Her shirt rolled up,
>>a lime in her mouth,
>>>a trail of salt
>>>>to her belly button
>>>>>overflowing with Patrón
>>>>>>(it is always Patrón).

A crowd instantly forms,
>cheers and howls from men
>>old enough to be her father
>>>taking pictures
>>>>offering their hands to help her off the bar
>>>>>offering to buy her another drink.

The Stock Exchange

Guys, boys, are a commodity.
　　Dating the trade,
　　　　New York City the floor.

Everyone is on the market
　　and there is a variety around to sample,
　　　　as I am looking for investment options.

Every person marketable in their own way.
　　Embracing arbitrage to get the most bang for their buck.

Each promotes their brand of New York City,
　　trying to impress
　　　　trying to drive up their valuation.

My portfolio is diverse,
　　exploring different sectors
　　　　to see which has the greatest yield.

The actors and models turn heads.
　　The bartenders can get you into any club.
　　　　The dancers can get you (standing room) tickets to any show.
　　　　　　The artists take you to all-you-can-drink gallery openings.
　　　　　　　　The lawyers take you to fancy dinners to prove they can afford to.
　　　　　　　　　　The architects show you all the classic details in your favorite dive.
　　　　　　　　　　　　The celebrities take you to apartments and hotels you will never afford
　　　　　　　　　　　　The label owners get you VIP passes at every venue.
　　　　　　　　　　　　The musicians get you on the guest list.
Yet, the first date volume doesn't yield a lot of second dates.

The market stays steady,
　　the exchange stays exciting
　　　　with new prospects IPOing every day.

Trades happen quickly,
　　freeing up capital to invest elsewhere.
Occasionally hiring friends as brokers
　　not relying on my own research.

The holidays always bring volatility to even the best bull market,
　　even your blue chips stop paying dividends
　　　　as we slowly edge toward a bear market until spring sets in
　　　　　　and everything starts to rally.

From East 10th Street, and Back Again

Your day starts at noon,
sun fills the apartment
blankets kicked to the floor hours ago.

Walk down Avenue B to Kate's Joint
coffee and the best tofu scramble in NYC.
Sit and read, until their lunch rush kicks in.

Walk to Atlas, the warm aged wood fills
the tiny space, resist the vegan desserts that look
like works of art, more coffee, and a place to write.
Black Tape blasts through your iPod.

As the sun starts to set, make your way uptown.
Or at least as uptown as you are willing to go.
Cross 14th street through Union Square
to 21st street until you are swallowed into Slate.
Always cool, even on the most humid days.

Wait until 10 pm, even on a Tuesday,
for it to come alive. Serve, drink, make
easy cash. Dance, flirt, become magnetic.

After your shift go to Snitch, Vela, Taj, Duvet.
Their bouncers know your bouncers
Never wait behind a rope or in a line.

Those clubs are never your scene though.
End up at Four Face Liar at 5 am.
and 7A at 8 am, finally eating dinner.

Walk home through Tompkins Square Park.
The sun is rising. The bums and addicts are still
groggy. The suits are on their way to their offices
about to be flooded in artificial light and broken dreams.

In your apartment, the sun just begins to filter in.
Lay down, fall asleep, soak up its warmth.

HiFi

I walk by the bars
    at noon on an August weekday
        air conditioning pours onto the sidewalk
            it gives me goosebumps as I pass.
The darkness is abrupt
    the bartender preps the bar for the night
        as the daytime drunks,
           the barflies,
               spill their worries.

II

I will always trade the suits in Ferragamo shoes for
    the scruffy guys in steel toed-boots.
        Always a refreshing respite from the bankers
        who believe they need to hold
            onto every cent they ever earned.

III

We always know one of our own.
    Bartenders, waiters, waitresses, hosts, and hostesses
        other service workers are clutch --
        low maintenance, tip well
            because we all know the three-dollar-an-hour hustle.

In a Starbucks on 6th Avenue

We meet in a Starbucks
    an hour before my waitressing shift.

Talk about all the things
    we think should be important.

Our hands awkwardly touching, maybe.
    But that doesn't really seem like
        something we would do.

We have been dating for over a year.
    We are attractive,
        this is convenient.

We are intertwined.
    We date other people,
        but never talk about it.

I went on a date with another actor,
    one that everyone knows and recognizes.

He is jealous.
    Not because we have real feelings for one another,
        but because we were trying to.
            Because he doesn't want to be second place
            and know it.

He pushes for a relationship.
    A traditionally defined
        exclusive one.

That neither of us want
    and both know won't work.

We try to force –
    We try to emulate –
        all those feelings we think
            we are supposed to have,
               that we are supposed to feel
               after dating for so long.

Slate, 4 am

After the lights are turned up
        then back down again,
after the doors are locked
        and curtains drawn,
the clubs and bars are filled with people
      who work at other clubs and bars.
The industry, we call it.

We spend all night
      running, pouring, hustling.
          We need to wind down
             before the sun comes up.

No cocktails, no mixers, no ice
      straight liquor or beer
         easy pour, easy clean.

The radio plays classic rock
      on the too expensive sound system
         as we talk,
            brag about sales,
                complain about shitty tables,
            gossip about who is sleeping with whom,
         as we play beer pong and pool,
      as we laugh and relax.

When the light creeps in
      through the heavy velvet curtains
         we take our cue -
            stumble out,
                eyes fight to adjust,
              catch a 7 am cab,
                  heading home among the suits
                   trudging to their offices.

Twenty First and Sixth Avenue, Please

Wake up
        Suffocated by the sun.
                Disoriented and groggy.
                        Chin throbbing.
                                Hand caked in blood.
Sit up.
        Stomach churns.
                Eyes focus.
                        Waitressing book on the table.
                                Open.
                                        Empty.
Stand up.
        One shoe on.
                Sock in my pocket.
Grope around for other injuries.
        No other spots of pain.
                No cuts or bruises or contusions.
                        The chin probably needs stitches.
                                A skull and crossbones bandage will have to do.

Still in my clothes from last night's shift.
        Only have an hour to get to work.
Brush my teeth.
        Put on makeup.
                Disguise the puffiness.
I have never been this hungover.
        Or maybe I am still drunk.
                Can you be both at the same time?

Grab keys from the floor.
        Hail a cab.
                There is no way I'm able to walk that far.
                        There is no way I'm able to stomach the smell of the subway.
                                Borrow $10 from the front desk against tonight's tips

Last night, we had a movie premiere.
        Sponsored by Patrón.
                Bottles and bottles and cases of free tequila.
                Leftover.
                        Not in the inventory.
                                Drank straight.
                                        By everyone.

21st between 5th and 6th

Dear Creeps,

This is to all of you I serve every day,
        every happy hour,
                every weekend—

To all of you who walk in
        with your chests puffed
            with your confident swagger
                with your cocky head tilt—
To those who are
        too touchy,
            too friendly,
                too pompous—

                            This is a bar, a pool hall, a dance club
                    I shouldn't have to remind your bachelor party
                not every bar is a strip club.

                        You should not ask your waitress or bartender
                    to remove any clothing
                or to join you for the rest of your night.
            Not even if you offer to pay her rent for a year.

                        I am not your baby, sweetheart, or honey.
                    You don't need to grab me to get my attention.
                You don't need to put your arm around my shoulder
            to give me your order.

And celebrities,
        musicians,
            athletes—
                You too.
                        Stop touching me.
                    It does not excite me.

            I am not your pawn.
                I am not here to be put on display.
                    I am not here to make you look important.
                            I am not part of your pitch.
                            I am not part of your show.
                                I am not part of your circus.

Vazacs

In a city full of loneliness
    we search for a connection
        no matter how momentary.

I am a waitress, a bartender, a regular.
    I meet a new batch of guys every day.

They ask me out,
    leave me notes,
        and phone numbers,
            have their friends talk them up.
                Most never catch on that it is my job to flirt.

There are New School pretty boys, SVA snobs, NYU brats
    and executives, label owners, and bankers.

There are cocky promoters and liquor reps
    and shy MTV crew guys.

There are designers who create art for famous video games
    and artists who haven't gotten their first solo show yet.

There are men who invite me to the opera
    and bros who invite me to the strip club.

There are recovering alcoholics who ask me out for coffee
    and bartenders who take me to after-hours underground bars.

There are Indie guys who make me mix CDs of bands that I will never listen to
    and aspiring actors who I will see as extras on Law & Order for years.

Always cautiously optimistic,
    always insisting we meet for drinks with no promise of dinner.

I avoid most goodnight kisses
    and offers to walk me home.
        Hoping they get the hint
            and won't have my address.

The actors and performers and bartenders are just as out of control as I am.
    The architects and accountants and lawyers make my eyes bleed.
        The video game designers and artists and musicians are too Brooklyn hipster.
        The sensitive guys never hold my interest.

Yet, we keep going out on the next date. With the next person.
    In this city of loneliness
        we continue to search
            for a connection
                that will last.

The MTA

It's December.
    It's below freezing.
        It's almost Christmas.

The buses and subways aren't running.
We are deep into day two of the transit worker's strike.

We walk the quiet streets
miss the hum of the subway

that usually reverberates deep in our bodies
grounding us to the pavement.

Trapped in Manhattan at 5 am
coworkers come by after closing Slate

with glasses of Patrón wrapped in cellophane
to celebrate the end of the strike.

No agreement has been reached
but NY1 reports that talks are going well

subway and bus service will be restored by
the morning rush hour.

We do not belong to that New York City,
deep asleep by the time the commuters start their day.

As the subway switches are tested
as the buses are gassing up

we sip Patrón until the sun rises
never once thinking about the implications

of a strike,
    of fair wages,
        of insurance,
            of a pension.

We are 22 years old
    making our rent
        not worrying about an undefined future.

On the books,
    making $3.33 an hour.

Off the books,
    the cash never stops flowing.

Ace

Not that I've had a lot of
One-night stands,

but, I've had a lot of
One-night stands.

Maybe it is the thrill of flirting.
Maybe it is being on the rebound.
Maybe it is the challenge and the conquest

of landing a guy you know
you have nothing in common with
but looks great in skinny jeans.

A guy who you don't want to talk to
but can't take your eyes off his lips.

A guy who is good for the night or the weekend
but who will fade into the morning.

Avenue A and 7th Street

Most nights are a blur.
    Not because of the fun I am having,
        but because of all the whiskey in my blood.

There are too many lost nights and fuzzy mornings,
                missing shoes and misplaced hoodies,
                        scraped knees and busted lips.

My brain shuts off –
    blocking out the embarrassments
        not willing to be in on the sabotage.
           Join in
                      or get run over.

I must be having fun though,
                right?
    In the pictures I am laughing,
     singing, dancing on the bar.

Drinking boys under the table,
    buying rounds of Patrón and Tabasco
        for anyone willing.

Too much whiskey, tequila,
    champagne saturating my body.

There are so many nights
    I shouldn't have made it home alive.

 Dumping my purse out
   on the sidewalk
     the only way to find my keys.

I never have any stories to tell, though.
    Most nights exist
        only in snippets of muddled moments.

Chelsea Girls

We all drink for different reasons.
    Reasons we all keep somewhere quiet.
      Reasons we never share.

I drink because
    I am always too much in my head.
      Thinking.
        Editing.
                Rewriting my story.

I drink because
    I was always the good kid.
      Self-conscious.
        Reserved.
                Never irresponsible.

I drink because
    I want to forget my
      heartbreak and
        disappointment.

I drink to get back at him.
    I am not the same girl he hurt
      when I am drowning in Jameson.
                He doesn't know that girl.

I drink to forget the path I have always been on
      to forget everything I expected of my life
        to forget everything we had planned.

I drink to
    outdo him on his level.

I drink to
    empower myself.

I drink because
    I crave recklessness.
      But that only happens after the third shot
        and minutes before the blackout.

I drink without regard
    for myself or
      anyone around me.

Fineline

I don't know when it started
    but I have been reinventing myself.

Slipping deeper and deeper
    into these New York years.

The drinking, the partying, the boys —
    they all stem from forgetting
        I am deadening the pain.

Trying to be more fucked up than you.
    To see if you notice.
        To see if you care.

You don't—
    until you think that I may have fucked a celebrity.

I want to call you.
    Tell you how much I miss you,
        but that the whiskey is doing a fine job
            of taking your place.

I get tattooed
    and pierced.
        I need the pain
            and the scars to remind me
                of what this is like
                    of what this feels like.

The Knitting Factory

I only see the changes
        when there are glimpses
                into my former life.
                        Nights at shows at Webster Hall
                                the Knitting Factory
                                        Arlene's Grocery
                                are lonely and fleeting.

I feel more connected
        once I meet up with my friends in a bar
                                        afterward.

None of my NYC crew know punk rock
        the pit
                the raw energy
                        the sweaty connection at a show.

Yet,
        it is the bar where I feel
                community now.

Manitoba's

Force the creativity.
Write in a coffee shop.
Move to a bar when the sun goes down.
Have another Jameson. Neat.
No chaser.
Forget about dinner.

Blurry faces and messy handwriting.
Maybe this is the phase, right before
the words start to flow.

The night becomes a black spot in your memory.
Moments come back in disjointed flashes.

The next morning,
        your notes, the words,
                are not made up of
                        any known alphabet.

The Hotel Chelsea, Room 126

She is a photographer
(who is still in school).
I am a poet,
(without any published poetry)
drinking too much whiskey
and reading too much Bukowski.
The Hotel Chelsea filled with ghosts
we hope to conjure.

Writer's block is a half myth.
I am writing, but it is garbage.
All telling. No showing. Self-indulgent. Rambling.
(Maybe I am reading too much Bukowski.)

At least at The Chelsea you can be
drunk and searching for your muse.
At least that is how all the legends go.
(Or maybe now, went, is the right tense.)

Room 126
lights, cameras,
red wine.

The after-party is a revolving door of friends,
drinking buddies, and the guys we are seeing.
We drink and laugh and shout in the hallways.

I wake up in the middle of the night.
Wide awake in the dark silence.
I step over the passed-out bodies scattered
on the crusty carpet and go to the balcony.
I sit on that concrete slab for hours,
staring at the city below me.
Lights in the apartment windows turn on and
off, people sauntering home from bars, buses
and cars heading somewhere.
Everyone moving moving forward forward.

I search for a connection.
Only 23 blocks from home.

Wall Street

He lives on Wall Street.
    Who the fuck lives on Wall Street?

It's cheap.
    No one wants to live that close
        to the World Trade Center
           when they are still finding remains
                on top of Trinity Church.

I take the 6 From Astor, transfer to the 4/5 at City Hall to Wall Street.
    Pass the guards armed with automatic weapons
        outside the stock exchange,
           convinced if I moved the wrong muscle
              I will be shot.
                      I tend to look mischievous.

The suits and their money have left
    with ticker tape stuck to their shoes.
The tourists and their cameras
    migrate back uptown for the bright lights of Times Square.

Deserted after 5:15 pm
    the neighborhood is ours.
        We get lost in those old streets
           that don't adhere to the grid,
              that are older than the revolution.
           Their cobblestone history
        their winding alleys
    their clapboard taverns
tucked away,
        waiting to be discovered.

The Sunshine Cinema

Among the drinking
    among the debauchery
        among the brashness,
            there is an innocence –

 on nights like these,
    when we walk out into the humid night,
        from the midnight show at the Sunshine
            I realize that we can be
                kids in any town
                    in any state,
                          almost –

From Chelsea to the Lower East Side

I never really want to go into the clubs –
the trendy ones with the lines, velvet ropes, and bouncers;
the ones with glass-topped bars and $14 cocktails; the ones with pulsing
music and LED lights; the ones with the DJs with the same tired rock set
(Sweet Child O' Mine, Livin' on a Prayer, and Pour Some Sugar on Me).
Tight skirts, high heels, and being surrounded by bros
was never my idea of a good time,
                    It is work,
                                and it pays well.

I'd much rather a dive –
one with a great jukebox and a bartender who buys
every fourth drink; the dark ones where the wooden bar
has been worn by spilled beer, drips of whiskey, and elbows;
the ones where I can read a book, talk about dead Russian authors,
suicidal poets, and punk rock legends.
            Those are the places,
                    where I am able to breathe.

Union Square East

The news,
    the murmurs in the streets,
        the steaming pavement -
           keep saying
               it is oppressively hot.

But that is not how it feels.
    I don't feel sticky
        or sweaty.

The power grid is straining,
    brownouts rolling across Manhattan
        change our atmosphere
           and give us new nuances
               electrifying our skin.

Union Square traffic lights are suspended,
    only headlights illuminating the sidewalks,
        skyscrapers are dim,
           the subway quiet.

Our favorite restaurants
    serve modified raw menus.
        Specials to push everything
           that can spoil.

We laugh with friends
    under candlelight
        drinking cocktails
           not missing
               the ice that melted hours ago.

Time is moving slower,
    we stop rushing from one place
        to the next,
               instead, we stretch out each

                        moment.

26th Street

Laying in bed with the streetlight shining in the window
covering us in orange light and casting the shadow
of the fire escape on the exposed brick wall.

The alarm goes off next door, fire trucks, flood the room red,
drunk voices shout, only barely rising to our window,
a garbage truck rumbles down the street.

Sticky and sweaty in the July night,
the sheet kicked off, crumbled, and knotted
at the foot of the bed.

The curtain hasn't moved in hours.
Breezes don't reach the fifth floor,
surrounded by high rises.

The sweat tastes salty when I kiss his temple.
His hand feels like fire as it moves to my thigh.

10009

Every New Yorker has their own take on the style of survival.

Oversized sunglasses and headphones –
    so you don't have to interact with the millions of people
        who are already invading your personal space.

Layers –
    scarves, jackets, sweaters.
        You will experience multiple climates per day.
            This will also help you move
                from the gym to coffee to work to drinks to an art show.

Large purse –
    book, phone charger, your discarded layers.
        You need a stylish bag to carry your life in.
            No cars here, everything is on your shoulder.

Change of shoes –
    make sure that there is room in your bag.
        You will not be running to catch the subway in your killer stilettos.

You will work too much.
    You will drink too much.
        You will care too much about where you eat and drink.

You will join a gym
    so you can continue eating and drinking
        at the right places.

You should find a friend who will not let you agree
    to go out with the bartender/ aspiring musician, actor, writer, filmmaker
        after your fourth drink.

Because you are all biding your time,
    until you make it big.

It is a game.
    You have to smile.
        You have to look good.
            You have to win.
                You have to make it out alive.

Astor Place to Union Square to Grand Central to Times Square

The rain tapers off
    into a misty drizzle
        washing away the day's tourists.

The city hums,
    neon flashes,
        cars surge --
            tires slap against the slick street,
                muffled sirens and whispers carry
                    from Times Square
              to the Lower East Side
        to the Bowery
      to Battery Park
    create the city's voice –
her cadence.

Lights blaze,
    echoes resonate,
        our heads whirl
           as we laugh
              and fall into each other.

Light refracts from the puddles
    making the streets
        and his face shimmer.

We dash
    from one conversation
        to the next,
           holding hands
            jumping in puddles.

Our spirits are stirred,
    excited
        to be here,
           in these streets,
              with wet jeans and soggy shoes.

A Terminated Lease

The Empire City

It all happened in a flash.
    Just like in the cartoons.
        It was an *oh shit* type of pain.

It was one shot of Jack that saved my life.
    Or at least a life that I could tell my mother about.
        It burned my whole body for three days.

I spent my early 20s drinking for free
    in the places people waited in line to get into.

Partying in VIP rooms
    with celebrities, rock stars, and athletes
        I didn't recognize (and a few I did).

The Jameson and Patrón and Veuve never ran out,
    there was always another comped bottle waiting to be popped,
        another round ordered,
            we were never cut off.

It was a blurry seductive world,
    where every night had the opportunity
        to be a one-night-only adventure, experience, story.

Nights of racing down the FDR in a convertible,
    of club hopping with Seth Green (and his dad),
        of doing shots with the Dell Dude,
            of riding on the back of a motorcycle,
                of comped concert tickets and backstage passes,
                    of premiere parties, after parties, and after after parties,
                        of bars that I could never find again when I sobered up,
                      of eating dinner at 7 am,

                                were always a possibility.

With every hangover I'd swear off alcohol,
    I swore I'd come home after my shift,
        every night I found myself heading to Four Faced Liar
        after we closed Slate
            waiting to see where the night would take me.

It was a cycle that I couldn't break away from,
    until that shot.
        It all happened in a flash --
           it was one shot of Jack that saved my life.

Avenue A

Those years exist in snippets
        of half-remembered nights.

Waking up late in the afternoon,
        hanging off my couch with only one shoe on,
                the stale taste of morning breath mixed with Jameson,
                        afraid to move, or my head will start aching.

Trying to piece the night back together,
        trying to fill those lost blocks of time,
                after the tower built of dripping rocks glasses turned into a mountain
                        before I invited everyone back to my apartment.

St. Mark's Place

I used to be a messy person.

Not the type of messy person who
    left laundry on the floor
        or dishes in the sink –

but the type of messy person
    who drank too much Jameson, Patrón , and pinot noir
        then ran around New York City.

The type of person whose friends
    were tired of looking after her.

I was careless with my body and friendships.
    I threw my heart around
        and let it bounce through dark streets
            soaked in whiskey and tequila.

I drank away regrets.
    I drank away any sort of genuine feeling.
        I drank to forget.

I burned bridges
    and scared people.

I was drowning
    but having a good time going under.
        Fuck it all.
            Living from moment to moment,
                acting on momentary desires.
                    We could die tomorrow,
                        live it up tonight.

I pushed everyone away,
    surrounded myself
        with people who were just as lost.
            Screw anyone else's feelings.
                I knew they'd be gone eventually anyway.
                    Friendships were reduced to drinking buddies
                      and brunch crews.

Together
    or alone –
        I could always find someone
          to pass the night with.

Avenue B, 2007

You like to think that something
    changes when you leave.

That somehow the landscape will be different.
That something would have sensed the moving truck and boxes
    and felt a loss, of something,
        of someone who had lived their life
                there for years.

But the street
    and the sidewalk
      remain the same.
Your apartment gets
    a fresh coat of paint and new renters.

Fingerprints on the doors and
    murals painted on the walls,
Scuff marks on linoleum and
    dents in the refrigerator door,
Beer caked in the carpets and
    wine stains in the sink ,
The laughter shouted from the rooftop and
    the crying on the fire escape,
Your blood dried on the pavement,
            all dissipate into the ether.
        Whitewashed,
     for the next tenant.

Life goes by
    on Avenue B
      like you were never there.

This street,
        this building,
          are all centuries older than you.
        Your stint is just a flash
    in their history.

In a city of such anonymity,
    years don't even add up to a footnote.

New York, New York

I moved to NYC
    dreaming of punk rock and starving artists.
      Rent and Jonathan Larsen,
          The Ramones and shows at CBGBs,
             The Hotel Chelsea and Allen Ginsberg.
         Of poetry readings at the Bowery Poetry Club,
      the Nuyorican Café, and St. Mark's Church.

Instead,
    I was stumbled into a world of drinking,
      celebrities, music executives,
         basketball players, label owners,
            and bottle service.
         The cash, the comps, the free drinks,
           skipping the lines, dates with actors –
         it was a world closer to Studio 54 and American Psycho.

It was all too easy,
          to turn down.

Avenue B, 300 sq. ft.

Those first nights gave us no indication
    of what was to come.

All we needed was that apartment,
    in that location,
        a roommate,
            first and last month's rent.

In that first apartment,
    an East Village pre-law tenement
        our TV sat on the floor
            as we watched *Empire Records* on repeat
                too broke for cable or a TV stand.

We went to school.
    We applied for jobs.
        We worked internships.
            Eventually able to afford a MetroCard and a bagel.

We sat on the fire escape
    and listened to the laughter from the Life Café garden
        while we imagined the breeze was reaching us.

We hung out on the roof
    and watched people with money go to bars and restaurants
        never feeling poor, never feeling behind. We were just waiting to ignite.

We didn't know then –
    the jobs we would get
        the celebrities we would meet,
            the clubs we would get into,
                the cash we would carry around.

We didn't know then
    that we would make it
        that we would be alright.

I suppose we all have to start from somewhere;
    our somewhere was a 5th-floor walk-up tenement
        with a tuberculous window.

B between 10th and 11th

I lived in that unheated
　　walk-up apartment for years.
　　　　Sharing a bedroom on the 5th floor
　　　　　　with a childhood friend.

Working multiple jobs –
　　waitress, bartender, gallery assistant, secretary,
　　　　on different schedules
　　　　　　while going to school,
　　　　　　　　just to stay in that apartment. Just to stay in New York City.

The bathroom walls were wallpapered
　　with my zero-dollar waitressing paychecks
　　　　and our beds were separated with homemade curtains.

My living room window led to the fire escape,
　　that fire escape led to the roof,
　　　　where I spent so many sunrises
　　　　　　and fireworks displays.

There must have been eight apartments
　　in that run-down tenement,
　　　　but, I had only ever met two of our neighbors
　　　　　　in all those years.
　　　　　　　　The couple across the hall
　　　　　　　　　　with the dogs
　　　　　　　　　　　　and the couple right below,
　　　　　　　　　　　　　　who would leave vegan muffins on our doorstep
　　　　　　　　　　　　　　　　after they fought too loudly. Sometimes with a note,
　　　　　　　　　　　　　　　　　　"Thanks for not calling the cops".

212

I wanted to have all of the New York City experiences
    I watched on TV and in movies and read about in books.
        I wanted to live the lives I saw in the movies and heard in songs.

                I wanted the innocence of Francie Nolan
                  and the opulence of Jay Gatsby;
                to live in a firehouse in Tribeca
            or in Lucy and Ricky's railroad apartment;
            a coffee shop like Central Perk
        and go to performances in vacant lots;
      to hang out with the next Warhol superstars
    with the next Television, the next Dictators, the next Beastie Boys;
collaborate with the next iteration of the Beats and the New York School;
befriend the ex-circus performers Maggie introduced me to, or even Maggie herself.

My apartment wasn't much more modern than the Kramdens',
    actually, it may have been smaller
        and it didn't help that we were two Oscars without a Felix.

Meow Mix closed before we got there
    but I did see some shows at CBGBs.

The Factories have all become apartments and office spaces
    and Max's Kansas City had been replaced by a series of cafés and caterers.

Skid Row had already been cleaned up
    and there was no place for Seymour or Audrey II.

I never made it up to 53rd and 3rd,
    and it was Zoltar in front of Gem Spa.

Coyote Ugly wasn't as rowdy as we hoped
    but we danced on the bar at Hogs and Heifers.

I never bought studded boots at Love Saves the Day
    but I did find the ring that Kate wears when she meets Dade.

I was friends with skaters and models,
    but none of them were victims of the AIDS crisis.

I spent a night in The Chelsea Hotel,
    but I didn't bleed out from an abdomen wound.

I never got into a cab with a Travis Bickle or Jim Ignatowski
    and I am sure that I missed Elvis Costello at a party once.

I laid flowers at Strawberry fields
    and peeked in the wrought iron gate of the Dakota,
        but never saw Yoko or a demonic cult.

I dated a guy who lived in Hell's Kitchen
      but he never sang Walk Like A Man.

I met several bankers
      who could have been stand-ins for Patrick Bateman.

Eric Neis is still around,
      alive, well, and in great shape.

I saw one opera and one ballet at the Met, Ethan Stiefel was even in it
      and Cabaret played at Studio 54.

Law and Order shoots were more regular than the subways
      and I lost count of how many extras I dated.

I had 2nd, 3rd, 5th, and 6th Avenue heartaches
      and the neon lights were still bright on Broadway.

I hung out in Tompkins Square, Washington Square, and Union Square
      but sometimes I felt positively 4th street.

I spoke conductor,
      had my own Bermuda Triangle sidewalk,
            and many, many pineapple incidents.

I never got arrested,
      so I still believe that all judges are like Harry Stone.

There were nights
      when it was an unfortunate time to be young
            and I dreaded I was becoming the fuck up.

There were days
      and weeks
            that I, too, felt like I was sitting under a bell jar.

I ate brunch at Life,
      but never danced on the tables singing protest songs.

The cadence of those days matched the frantic energy of *Howl*
      and we all felt like we were going to live forever.

We searched and destroyed,
      and learned that dreaming is free.

I never had a personality crisis
      or dreamed of ending up like Sweet Jane.

I was part of a new Blank Generation
      living my own fairytale of New York.

The whole time, singing along,
      "If you can make it here, you can make it anywhere".

The City

We knew the city would have our backs.
    We were part of it.
        It looked out for us.
            Gave us some of its magic.

We wandered the streets late at night into the early morning
        with the excitement of discovery
            of stumbling on something that could only happen here
                someone who can only live here
                    something we can only see here.

Nursing my shift drink, Jameson neat, when he walked in,
a friend of a friend of a friend. We race up the West Side Highway,
through the quiet streets of the Upper East Side in a convertible
and down the FDR to Alphabet City for stiff drinks at Mona's.

        I get on the back of his baby blue Honda without a second
        thought, on the second day he owns it. 125 miles from NYC to
        Wilkes Barre, PA and back again to open the diner at sunrise.

            We enter the Chinese restaurant at the basement level, guided
            through a subterranean labyrinth, almost hitting our heads on pipes
            and duct work. We emerge into a room, radiating, lit with lanterns and tea lights,
            sit in the corner, flames flickering on our faces, drinking flasks and cups of sake.

                He is a regular at Slate when he is in town filming. After a few visits and
                Kamikaze shots, he asks me out. We go to dark clubs. Run into Jake
                Gyllenhaal. We dance. We go to another club. And another. Then to a
                loft I will never afford. We sneak into a hallway. He fumbles to kiss me.

                    Our first date continues into the next morning as he walks
                    me home. Wall Street to the East Village. We don't rush, or run
                    for cover when the January rain starts. We walk slowly through
                    the neighborhoods, named to numbered to lettered streets.

                      Energized and exhausted walking through the Chelsea streets leaving
                      the Rocky Horror Picture show at 2 am when I crash into Taye Diggs
                      and he so gallantly apologized to me. Idina Menzel just laughs.

The city gave us
        Mondo Kim's to discover everything we only heard about in our small towns,
            that first edition in a pile of $1 books from an Astor Place street vendor,
                the 45 I had been looking for years at Loves Saves the Day, for a quarter,
                    and especially, that apartment two doors down from the Life Café
                                    in my price range.

We were part of its fabric,
        we dressed up for the Halloween parade,
            we made ourselves up with its dirt and soot,
                we wore its dark alleys and neon lights like a cloak.

We cursed its movie sets altering our commutes.
    We wrote, and performed, and skated in its parks.
        We worked, we hustled, we persevered, just to live here.

We knew the city would have our backs,
    and it always did.
        Always.

From the FDR to the West Side Highway

We worked –
        we drank –
            we roamed –
                trying to discover something new
                    trying to discover if we were who we always wanted to become.

We never stood still for long
    maybe we were terrified
        we would start to become stale
            maybe we hoped
                our movement would help us catch fire.

We raced through those years
    with no abandon
        with no second guessing
            with the naivety that feeds dreams
                and poems
                    and memoirs
                        and nostalgia.

The East Village

Even after ten years –
    fifteen years   away –
Every time I walk on those streets
    I feel like I am home.

I had walked every street
    and every avenue for so many hours
        for so many years.

The back alleys, shortcuts through parks, and
    dead ends in the projects
        in Alphabet City, where they abandoned the grid.

Wandering by myself
    discovering their secrets
        and hidden nuances.

I walk down Avenue B, past the empty Life Café space,
    past the former Lakeside Lounge –
        to my old front door.
            The door is new, the graffiti is new,
                and I bet the lock works now too.

The bodega is still on the corner,
    I wonder if the same man still works there.
        We never knew each other's names,
            but I like to think that we were looking out for one another.
            He always sat stoically behind the counter,
                open all night,
                    no bulletproof glass.
                        A 24-hour beacon of necessity.

7B is standing,
    but the jukebox has become subpar.
The Joe Strummer mural outside of Niagara has been touched up.
    It's now so bright that it looks out of place
        or maybe the issue is that it looks like it fits right in.

Before all the well-lit, modern Chinese food
    it was St. Mark's, tattoo shops, head shops,
        Trash & Vaudeville, Gem Spa,
            stores where any small-town kid
                could buy punk clothes from bands
                    that broke up before she was born.
                        All the studded belts, Manic Panic hair dye, and
                            t-shirts she had been searching for.
    The stores and the band names have changed
        but at least you can still get tattooed and pierced at
            any time of the day or night.

Ray's has stayed the same thanks to all the community support,
    but I still crave BurritoVille's vegan burrito.
Around the Clock is now a boutique bakery,
    Alt is a health food store,
Lakeside closed and
    its photo booth is seeking a new bar to call home.
No one has moved into the old Life Café space,
    Kate's Joint didn't make it, even with all the remodels.
Odessa is unrecognizable.
    Old Devil Moon has faded from the neighborhood's memory.

Yet I can still see,
    their old signage,
        remember their décor
            remember how it felt to be part of the community
                who frequented, who worked, who ate, who drank, within their walls.
I can still hear the laughter
    and the murmur of separate conversations joining together,
smell the carrot ginger dressing, the coffee,
    taste the mimosas, the whiskey, and the unturkey club,
        feel the beckoning glow
            of familiarity, of my neighborhood.
As I knew it.
    As I loved it.

Even with this ever-changing landscape
    of bars and restaurants and coffee shops
        where I used to be a regular
            where I used to know the staff and other regulars
            where I used to be the staff
                I get a twinge of nostalgia.

Crust punks still mix with bums mixing with the
    young professionals walking their dogs to Tompkins Square Park.
Kids still skateboard in Union Square
    and you may have to jump a deck
        as you race to catch a train.
The sun still sets behind the same buildings
    where the water ice man still wheels his cart
        of syrup in re-purposed liquor bottles,
            music still bellows from open windows and fire escapes.

                But none of it is mine anymore.
            It belongs to another generation of young artists—
                kids trying to make their dreams a reality
      as they toil at day jobs as waitresses, bartenders, baristas
            and paint, write, perform at night.
The streets of
    Alphabet City,
        The East Village,
            the Lower East Side,
                wherever the divide is today –
                    They still feel a little bit like home.

Gotham

How can one city hold so many ghosts?
    My own –
        and those whose paths
                                         I never crossed.

Hundreds of years
    building and rebuilding
        moving forward
            wiping away the years, the people, the legends.

But the grit, the history, the dreams
    still persist
        still endure
            still electrify the streets
                for the next generation.

8 Stuyvesant Street

I can almost see all their faces
　　yet they never quite come into focus.

The regulars—
　　The ones who always tipped well,
　　　　the ones who made fantastic conversation,
　　　　　　the ones who made your shift go a little faster.

Around the Clock was a neighborhood diner.
　　Filled with students, professors, people who lived
　　　　in the East Village for years and decades
　　　　　　and those who just arrived.

There was the professor, her untamed curly hair, her quick, gruff cadence
　　let you know she had been a part of the neighborhood
　　　　when it was still something to be a part of.
I don't remember her real name or even what she drank
　　but my first week in NYC she taught me to be a New Yorker –
　　　　You never refer to 6th Ave as Avenue of the Americas.　　Ever.

Adrien was a two-beer guy. Amstel Light.
　　His face was young but his temples were grey.
　　　　I often saw him out, at other bars, on a schedule
　　　　　　making his way west, two Amstel Lights at a time.

The atmosphere in the diner changed when Marcel walked in.
　　Kind eyes, soothing accent, an artist's attention
　　　　a Buddhist's aura. He wore his soul on his sleeve.

There were the NYU kids who invited me to college parties
　　and left a handwritten goodbye note when they graduated.

Margaret who did a crossword puzzle
　　over a cup of coffee for hours every Tuesday night.

The bus driver and his sister
　　who came in for breakfast every night at 1 am after his shift.

The quiet artist who left me Sharpie sketches
　　of the other customers with my tip.

The singer from H20,
　　who never knew I recognized him.

The two gamers in black trench coats who
　　it took me months to break through their shyness.

The impossibly beautiful group of twenty-somethings
　　who never missed a Sunday brunch.

The two old men who met at the diner once a week
>> and I always feared for the Saturday when one of them
>>> would be stood up.

Over the years, their faces have blurred together
>> and their names had faded.
>>> Some I saw every day
>> some once a week
>> some only when they were passing through New York.
But we created a routine for one another,
> a sense of familiarity
>> in a city so void,
>>> so desperate
>>>> for human connection.

Manhattan

There are a few memories
    that still make me smile
        with that sense of nostalgia.

It was being months away from stability
    and having the cash that gave me the time to drink too much.
        It was before I was on the inside.

It was before I was single
    and before I met the boy from the band.
        It was an innocent time of scrambling, saving, cutting corners.

It was shots of Patrón , Jameson neat,
    and comped bottles of champagne.
It was always Veuve or Moët.

It was skipping the line
    with a nod from the bouncer.
        It was never waiting behind a velvet rope.

It was dancing on bars and doing body shots
    in clubs that will be shuttered by the next year.
        It was laughing all night.

It was the industry
    and drinking in after-hours spots until sunrise.
        It was being on the inside.

It was a Burning Angel party at a Boy's Room
    and a drag queen named Peppermint.
        It was hanging out at gay clubs with androgynous beauties.

It was dark dive bars on a Tuesday night
    with the best jukeboxes in New York City.
        It was $2 Tecate and tequila shot specials.

It was Sunday brunch
    with dark glasses and mimosas.
        It was day drinking and stumbling home at 6 pm.

It was midnight movies at The Sunshine
    and *The Rocky Horror Picture Show* in Chelsea.
        It was summer nights away from the bars.

It was the Halloween parade
    and West 4th street.
        It was the best vegan wings in Manhattan.

It was dinners of leftovers from a party buffet
    eaten straight from a take-out container with a stolen fork.

It was stopping at a bodega at 3 am for a piece of fruit.

It was a trophy door
    wallpapered with scraps of paper with boys' phone numbers.
        It was getting at least one phone number per shift.

It was working doubles
    and pushing food that was about to expire.
        It was upselling drinks to people who couldn't taste a difference.

It was avoiding NYU properties after snow storms
    because they never shoveled their sidewalks.
        It was how NYU kept moving east.

It was standing in line to enter the lottery for Rent tickets
    and seeing it from the front row.
        It was taking everyone who visited.

It was a winter of *Black Tape* blaring through ear pods
    and a summer of *American Idiot.*
        It was the accidental destruction of so many iPods.

It was getting tattooed
    and pierced.
        It was becoming vegan.

It was running down the street
    screaming *I Feel Like Making Love.*
        It was dumping my purse out on the sidewalk to find my keys.

It was a magical time to be young and drunk
    with no fear or boundaries.
        It was always bouncing back.

It was being twenty-one
    and indulging in excess.
        It was being invincible.

It was not being ready to leave,
    but the city becoming something different.
        It was changing without you.

It was throwing myself head-first into those days,
        into everything
                with no abandon.

ABOUT THE AUTHOR

Andrea is a mess of contradictions, fan of parallel structure, and nostalgic pack rat who writes poetry about punk rock kids and takes photos of forgotten places. She believes in the beauty of the ordinary, the power of the vernacular, and the history of the abandoned. Through her work, she strives to prove that poetry can be dirty, gritty, and accessible by revealing the art in what we see, say, do, ignore, and forget every day.

Raised by rock and roll parents, she learned the importance of going to concerts and ignoring the "no trespassing" signs in her childhood. She spent her adolescence in a small town punk rock scene where she moshed, fell in love, and produced a few cut-and-paste zines, before escaping to New York City and causing a ruckus in Alphabet City. After meeting her husband in one of those Chelsea bars she has settled in Pittsburgh, is at the whim of a feisty terrier, works in tech, and still prefers Jameson neat.

After paying a few universities way too much tuition, they granted her several degrees in creative writing. When her education was complete, she started garnering some publishing credits, including a sold out run of Mix Tapes and Photo Albums: memories from a small town scene.

She is uncomfortable talking about herself, even in third person.

www.andreajanov.com